D0853759

MIGHTY MOVERS

Trains

A Buddy Book
by
Sarah Tieck

ABDO
Publishing Company

VISIT US AT
www.abdopub.com

Published by ABDO Publishing Company, 4940 Viking Drive, Edina, Minnesota 55435.

Copyright © 2005 by Abdo Consulting Group, Inc. International copyrights reserved in all countries. No part of this book may be reproduced in any form without written permission from the publisher. Buddy Books™ is a trademark and logo of ABDO Publishing Company.

Printed in the United States.

Written and Edited by: Sarah Tieck
Contributing Editor: Michael P. Goecke
Graphic Design: Maria Hosley
Image Research: Sarah Tieck
Photographs: Freefoto.com, Michael P. Goecke, Gopher State Railway Museum, Photos.com, Michael Reeve
Special thanks to the Science Museum of London.

Library of Congress Cataloging-in-Publication Data

Tieck, Sarah, 1976-
   Trains / Sarah Tieck.
       p. cm. — (Mighty movers)
   ISBN 1-59197-830-0
       1. Railroads—Juvenile literature. I. Title.

TF148.T54 2004
385—dc22
                                                            2004050228

Table of Contents

What Is A Train?

A train is a line of railroad cars that moves on tracks. A locomotive pulls the train into the station. The locomotive is a special car at the front of the train. It holds the train's engine.

The train's conductor shouts, "All aboard!" He or she helps people and checks freight. His or her job is to make sure the train trip is smooth.

The engineer drives the train. He or she knows railroad signals and rules, and how to run the locomotive.

The locomotive pulls the train along tracks.

The conductor and the engineer are a part of the train's **crew**. The engineer drives the locomotive, which is the first car. The rest of the crew rides in the caboose. This is the last car of the train.

An engineer climbs into the locomotive.

The caboose is the last train car.

What Do Trains Do?

Trains have many uses. People ride them. Businesses use them to carry things. Trains save money, time, and work.

People ride passenger trains to work.

Trains carry freight across the country.

PARTS OF A TRAIN

Warning bell

Headlight

Locomotive number

4501

4501

Warning bell

Cowcatcher

Steam whistle

Cab

Tender car

Dining car

Flanged wheels

How Trains Work

An electric train uses electricity. This electricity comes from a power line's electric current. An "arm" on the train touches power lines above or beside the track. The electricity from the power line runs through the "arm." This makes the train move.

Trains also run on diesel engines. A diesel engine uses fuel. The fuel burns inside the engine and makes electricity. This moves the train.

This train uses electricity to move.

Steam engines run on the power of hot steam. The crew builds a fire in the locomotive's furnace. This heats up a part called the boiler, which holds water. As the water boils, it makes steam. The steam moves the parts of the engine.

The crew uses coal to build a fire.

Hot steam makes the train smoke.

Trains Today

Most trains today use electric or diesel power. These types of fuel are cleaner and make the train move faster. Steam trains are still used in China and India. In the United States, people ride them to learn about history and have fun.

Subways, monorails, and more traditional trains carry goods and people. New and old trains are a link in the world's transportation system.

People ride trains and subways.

The Story Of Trains

1550s—The first freight trains were wagons that ran on parallel boards. This machine made work easier. It was used in Europe's mines.

1800s—Horses provided the power for most railroads around the world.

1804—Richard Trevithick was first to use steam engines to pull freight along a track.

1808—The first steam engine ran in London. The track was shaped like a circle. The train was called, the "Catch me who can."

1823—George Stephenson began building steam locomotives for countries around the world. He was called the "father of railways."

1830s—People started riding on trains. By the 1850s, most passenger trains had heat, light, toilets, and food.

1850s—Most trains ran on steam power. This time period was known as the "age of steam."

1869—Train tracks stretched across the United States. This helped the United States to grow.

1879—The first electric trains were invented by Werner von Siemens. They ran from power in an electric line above the train. Many trains today are electric.

1893—Dr. Rudolph Diesel introduced the diesel engine. Many trains switched from steam power to diesel power.

Famous Trains

Puffing Billy

Today, this is one of the oldest steam locomotives in the world. In 1813, this train car pulled coal wagons in England.

Peruvian Central Railway

This railroad train, which debuted in 1895, is considered the highest in the world. It travels from Callao, Peru, and climbs 13,000 feet (3,962 m) to cross the Continental Divide.

Puffing Billy is on display at the Science Museum of London.

Flying Scotsman

This was a famous express train in the 1920s. It traveled almost 400 miles (644 km) between London, England, and Edinburgh, Scotland.

The Flying Scotsman today.

Important Words

Continental Divide a stretch of land that runs from Canada to South America.

crew a group of people who work together.

diesel engine an engine that uses fuel for power.

engine a machine that creates energy to make something run or move.

Europe the continent between Asia and the Atlantic Ocean. England, France, and Italy are some of the countries in Europe.

freight the goods carried by a train.

parallel lying side by side.

passengers the people who ride a train.

railroad a system of tracks used by train cars for transportation.

steam engine an engine that uses boiling water for power.

transportation how things move from one place to another.

Web Sites

To learn more about trains, visit ABDO Publishing Company on the World Wide Web. Web site links about trains are featured on our Book Links page. These links are routinely monitored and updated to provide the most current information available.

www.abdopub.com

Index